Generous Moments

Generous Moments

Snapshots of Goodness on Ordinary Days

Catherine C. Pike

Illustrations by Alison A. Buchanan

With joy —

Cathie Pike

Rosebrook Publishers

Rosebrook Publishers
P. O. Box 1003
New Canaan, CT 06840-1003

Text by Catherine C. Pike
Illustrations by Alison A. Buchanan
Edited by Constance D. Kissling
Photograph by Dorcas A. Casey
Design by Northeastern Graphic, Inc.
K M I Keith W. McGinnis, Inc.

First Edition Printed in China 2004

10 9 8 7 6 5 4 3 2 1

Library of Congress Cataloging-in-Publication Data

ISBN (Hard Cover) 1-932203-26-5
ISBN (Soft Cover) 1-932203-27-3

*In loving memory of my mother and father,
Betty and Bill Crawford, who lived lives of quiet
and abundant generosity.*

Moments

Preface

*G*enerous Moments tells of the warmth and diversity of goodness done by ordinary people on ordinary days, often in extraordinary ways. Stories, suggestions, family memories, and personal experiences I've encountered have been woven into a collage of generosities throughout the chapters. The *Moments* are short impressions, like snapshots, taken of people serving people in everyday life.

My niece suggested the book topic to me as we walked on a Thanksgiving afternoon. I remember the bend in the road when she said emphatically, "Well, the book you should be writing is about generosity." Within hours I began the book, and it's been a pleasure to write. Inspiration for many of the stories came from good friends, interesting strangers, and my wonderful family whose acts of kindness continually add new dimensions to the word *generosity*.

I hope *Generous Moments* awakens your awareness of gestures of thoughtfulness that occur near you every day.

Acknowledgements

*F*riendships bloom in many ways. My friendship with Connie Kissling has grown for years in our garden of words. As editor and friend, Connie helped bring *Moments* to print. My sincere gratitude will always belong to her.

My grateful appreciation also is extended to Keith McGinnis who contributed thoughtful and patient guidance in the process of publishing my first book.

With gladness, I thank my niece, Dorcas Ann, who gave me the spark that began this project about generosity.

For the wonderful stories inspired by friends and family, especially Lisa, Dan, Bob, Ashleigh, and Bill, I am very thankful. Their examples of generosity provided the vital spirit of *Generous Moments* and many will find a touch of their lives within the pages.

Quiet Gestures

Everyone's Heart
Small Wave
Stay with Us
Enlarge the Circle
Give Five
Caring Touch
A Back Rub
To the Cook
Go Ahead in Line
Proclaim a Day
Smile
Flowering the Visits

Everyone's Heart

*T*here it was coming toward us: a big, yellow school bus, adorned with a bright, red heart on the chrome grid. The bus driver gave the town a surprise on that cold, snowy morning in February. Originally it may have been planned as a gift for his little passengers, but, in reality, the traveling Valentine made everyone on the road smile.

Kind acts for a few people, to our surprise, often touch many. It happened with one heart on a school bus spreading cheer to a community.

Small Wave

*L*ittle ones sense sadness and react in their own little ways. The granddaughter of a friend had been busy chasing pigeons in Central Park when she noticed a very sad looking man on a bench. At the innocent age of one and a half, she walked right up to his face and waved. It was a small queen's wave, back and forth. He lifted his head from his hands and smiled. The smile grew bigger each time she passed him. Did her gentle attention stir an inner pool of happiness to change his day?

Stay with Us

As I listened to a friend's pain one night, all I could think to offer was our extra bedroom. "If at any moment you are overcome, jump in the car and come stay in our home. The extra bed is there for you at any hour; just use the key. If you come in the middle of the night, leave us a note on the stair, 'I'm in the guestroom'."

When someone experiences tragedy, friends and family rally around for the first few weeks. Then quiet, cold reality slips in the door. For many, the word "loneliness" becomes *modus operandi*.

Our friend never came, but she often thought of it and said that it was one of the kindest gestures after her husband's death.

Enlarge the Circle

---

*J*ust open your hands, pick up the phone, and invite a newcomer into your circle. It is tough moving to a town where all the circles are closed.

Our family experienced many thoughtful gestures when we relocated to another state. New acquaintances included us in neighborhood gatherings, parties, popular town celebrations, after-school events, and club memberships. They suggested doctors, dentists, schools, sports-camps, specialty shops, and on and on. Weekly they shared general information about the area. Because they enlarged circles to include us, their kindness made all the difference in our four-year visit. It opened new doors of adventure to every member of our family, and we were very grateful for their welcome.

When returning to visit these friends, I often feel I am grabbing a rainbow of permanent colors. The new friendships begun years ago haven't washed away.

Give Five

*I*t takes about five seconds to wave a stranger into the space ahead of you. Traffic slows for a moment. A wave flashes in the windshield and "thank you" is uttered, but not heard. A momentary peace fills your car, while a total stranger is grateful to finally enter the flow of traffic going home. Give five.

A Caring Touch

*T*ake the time. Sit quietly. Touch someone who is ill at home or in the hospital. A touch on the arm, a kiss on the forehead, a held hand gives special comfort. These gentle gestures make patients feel loved, in spite of their unbecoming state. People, who hustle about actively from morning 'til night, may not think small acts like this matter much, but in the long days of discomfort, a caring touch is gold.

A Backrub

Give a backrub. Even the thought elicits the sensation of relaxation, a panacea for a stressful day.

Some say that the way to a man's heart is through his stomach with good food. But, as a child, I scratched my brother's back for hours and I'm sure that's what placed me permanently in his heart.

A backrub or a backscratch creates good moments for others. It's often a generous gesture done by someone who has many other more pressing things to do.

To the Cook

*T*here's praise in the words, "Mom, that was a delicious dinner." And, "You must have done something differently; I think these were your best pancakes ever." Twenty-eight years, same recipe, same pancakes, wonderful enthusiasm! There's even appreciation in the short sentence, "Thank you for dinner."

Guests thank hostesses, people thank strangers, but it's the daily cook who needs a generous thank you for ordinary meals. "Goodbye" or "I'm going to do my homework now" could be accompanied by "Thanks. That was good." Such words ease kitchen cleanup and give the feeling that a big hug has been placed upon the table.

Why do we take a cook for granted? Little-ones, teens, middle-aged and older, everyone can sing praises to the cook! That's generosity.

Go Ahead in Line

Many folks read magazine covers and newspaper headlines while they stand in the grocery checkout line; others read people. Some faces display a clock ticking. Working people and mothers of young children have so much to do in so little time that standing with five items behind someone with thirty can increase the stress thermometer to uncomfortable heights. "Please go ahead. I have plenty of time," is a generous offer to a stranger.

Proclaim a Day

*I*f you are inspired one morning to proclaim the day, Daughter's Day, Grandson's Day, Great Aunt's Day or Son-in-Law's Day, just proclaim it. Write a card or letter to the special someone expressing your excitement and reasons for the declaration. It should be easy. The sentiments will flow because you have chosen the date; it wasn't designated by a card company or a national committee.

I wrote my daughter recently and above the date I scripted *Daughter's Day* in large elegant letters. She phoned, "Is it really Daughter's Day?" "Well," I remarked, "I thought you deserved an original day, and so I proclaimed it. It's Daughter's Day for you."

Mother's Day, Father's Day, and Secretary's Day are popular, but we can also set aside a special day for a special person close to us. Being thanked and praised in a unique way for being wonderful would please anyone.

Smile

"I can hear your smile," said someone on the phone. "It started all the way down in your heart." I was surprised; she couldn't see me.

A smile carried in a voice makes a personal connection. A happy picture travels across miles and brings cheer and humor. Keep smiling, even when you can't be seen.

And keep smiling when you can be seen. You have no idea who is catching the love.

At the end of a school year, a small child wrote a thank you note to the school nurse. It said simply: Thank you for always smiling when you gave me my medicine. To her those daily smiles must have radiated an amazing amount of kindness.

Flowering the Visits

When a daughter moved her mother into a senior residence, several towns away, she began a weekly gift of flowers. Each time she visited she carried a bouquet in her hands. While her mother watched, she arranged, and they chatted. They both loved gardening, and this friendly interchange happened week after week for almost seven years. What loving devotion was nestled in this quiet pleasure!

As her mother's health faded and she went from apartment to assisted living to full-time care, she always had flowers decorating her room. It was a soothing presence for them both. The daughter explained, "It left a bit of me there in her room once a week." The giver, the receiver and the nurses all received pleasure from the arrangements.

The mother soon connected the fresh cut flowers to a visit from her daughter. Even as she slipped into Alzheimer's, she kept the connection: flowers, daughter, visit, love. The flowers tied everything in her world together.

The daughter remembers the warm visits and the cheerful bouquets. It's a memory that pleases.

Generous Gifts

Silver Bracelet

Flavor the Move

One Charm

Unexpected Soft Animals

First Day Bouquet

Passing Trains

Gifts on the Hour

The Reindeer Run

Many Films

Upbeat or Quiet Cool

Beautiful Handwork

Remember Teachers

The Silver Bracelet

Children learn early that it is fun to give presents to others. One day I noticed my silver bracelet wrapped up in tissue paper with a lovely bow sitting on my dresser. My second grader explained that she intended to give it to her favorite bus driver as a gift. Not wishing to squish her big heart, I suggested that maybe the driver didn't wear silver and perhaps a pretty pad and pencil would be just right. The bus driver enthusiastically accepted the useful gift, never knowing what else had been wrapped up for her, and my daughter received the joy of giving a surprise.

Children are very creative in their forms of generosity.

Flavor the Move

Giving a basket of memberships will instantly enrich a relative's life when she moves to a new town. Arrange memberships to museums and galleries, gardens and area attractions, the historical society and the library. Give a subscription to the local newspaper. If possible, make available dual memberships so she can invite new friends to happenings.

As the mailbox fills with interesting local opportunities, the basket of surprises creates a sense of welcome. This generosity will give a flavorful start to her new life and the following year she can renew her favorite memberships.

One Charm

A grandmother took all the charms off her gold bracelet with a plan to pass them along to her daughters, daughter-in-law and granddaughters. She invited the relatives to come for tea at separate times. As each one chose a charm from a velvet tray, she told where the charm came from and why it was special to her. It was a personal way to pass along the treasured charm bracelet and stories of her life.

Generosity can be giving our possessions away while we are alive and can see the new owners enjoy them.

Unexpected Soft Animals

When a twenty-something needing surgery and an elderly aunt in a nursing home were given similar get-well presents, they may have thought the giver a bit wacky. Both were well beyond treasuring stuffed animals, but both found diversion in their soft gifts.

The twenty-something received a big, floppy, scrumptious dog that he moved around his apartment. It slept on his pillow, at the foot of the bed, and on the sofa as he watched videos during his recuperation. Dog was a good companion.

The aunt opened her gift box and instantly clasped the pair of monkeys onto her wheelchair. They took on a bit of a life and became conversation pieces with the other residents. She and her "monkey friends" were inseparable, and they gave her more joy than owning another sweater or scarf.

Sometimes the unexpected gesture placed in a box makes a surprisingly successful present.

First Day Bouquet

Changing jobs was difficult. Moving thousands of miles away to start the new job multiplied the difficulty. Then a surprise arrived.

Midmorning, on the first day of work, a large bouquet of flowers was delivered to her desk. The card read, "You're a Superstar. You'll be missed, but we send great wishes for your new job. From your former colleagues."

After a moment of shock, she visualized the group and felt their spirit of enthusiasm for her new venture. What an exceptional gift from a past employer who did not want to lose her!

Passing Trains

An older uncle had extensive sets of trains that filled a room with excitement when they were all on full throttle. But, he had a dilemma. He had no children and he needed to move. What should he do with the trains?

A lucky nephew had just become a parent. He was building a house and could plan to devote a room to the train sets. What serendipity for a young family! The uncle gave him his collection and only asked that he come pack them himself. It took almost a week to unwire, detach, wrap and box each part, and then drive them halfway across the country.

Someday the nephew's son will grow into them, but until then, the trains will be popular with guests a bit older. Also, they could make a grand attraction to raise money for a community charity; it would be generosity on the move, passing from uncle to nephew and then to a good cause.

Gifts on the Hour

---

*C*hildren need distractions on long trips. Parents try to be creative. Years ago on every airline trip, a parent gathered assorted quiet games, coloring books and amusements to help her children pass the time. The gifts were individually wrapped and tucked in small bags decorated with popular animals. On the hour, the children eagerly opened and enjoyed the activities.

Twenty-five years later, the mother-daughter team planned another vacation. The mother had completely forgotten the survival kit habit, but her daughter had not. She had wrapped surprises. As they flew, she handed small gifts to her mother. First, came the gummy bears, then hand cream, and goodies every hour.

It is a special moment when children remind us of their good memories.

The Reindeer Run

*T*eachers constantly think out of the box in unique and generous ways to encourage children mentally and physically.

One teacher, an outstanding athlete, had found many pleasures connected with running. Running offered a definite goal, the friendship of fellow runners, and a sense of respect. It required little equipment and took place outside, which made her feel good. She decided to organize an event for her inner-city elementary school children to experience the same pleasures—The Reindeer Run.

All ages from kindergarten through fifth grade were welcome to enter The Reindeer Run one afternoon in December. There were boys races and girls races around the playground and the lengths varied according to grades.

The starter was the teacher's father; he wore a Santa hat. Her mother helped hand out frozen turkeys or pies to the first, second, and third place winners in every race. What excitement to carry a turkey or dessert home, kindly donated by a local supermarket! Every child received a tee shirt and every child was a winner when he or she joined The Reindeer Run. When the teacher moved, it became The Bunny Hop in April. Same spirit of generosity! Same run for fun!

Many Films

Some presents give unexpected delight. A young couple sent a photo album, a grandpa picture frame, and eighteen rolls of film as a gift to a favorite uncle because his first grandchild was coming to visit. Eighteen rolls seemed extremely generous. But, they were instantly put to use, and, in one week's time, the new grandparents had shot thirteen rolls—312 pictures! What seemed an extravagant gift became a perfect one. Every action of the precious new grandchild was recorded because there was film to spare. The family laughed at the grandparents' exuberance, but they all love the finished album.

It's delightful when relatives think of other relations and out-of-the-blue send a present.

Upbeat or Quiet Cool

*I*f we enjoy music played on guitars, drums, saxophones, and other instruments by live musicians in dusty subway areas or on hot, windy streets, perhaps we should pass some money from our pockets to theirs. They usually offer their talents for these quick concerts in locations that are never glamorous, but where a daily audience walks by. And their instrumental music adds a good beat to our day.

Other spontaneous performers sing for us with voices that sound like cool water being poured softly over the earth. It's a calming gift. Every bill in the hat encourages more music for people moving along in a busy world. However, those with songs in their hearts would probably still share their generosity and play somewhere, sometime, even if no one pays.

Beautiful Handwork

Faithful members who create beautiful handwork for their churches are blessings to a congregation. These men and women are like angels: they suddenly appear with gifts in their hands or new ideas in their heads to beautify the interior and exterior of church buildings.

In free time, parishioners patiently needlepoint kneelers and cushions, appliqué banners and wall hangings, and embroider altar cloths for churches. Others create magnificent sculptures, paintings, and stained glass windows. These artistic expressions enhance the liturgical experience in places of worship. Fortunately, dates and names or initials are usually sewn or added in some way to give a provenance about the pieces for future members.

So many works of art that adorn churches are overlooked. The designs and religious symbols are seen, but not really seen. It would be grand if there were a way to increase awareness and enlarge everyone's love for the beautiful handmade treasures.

Remember Teachers

Write a note of appreciation to a teacher, a coach, or a counselor. Because they put large hearts into their work for children and young people, many deserve special acknowledgement. A generous gift is communication expressed on paper and placed in an envelope.

Days after writing a distinguished teacher to express understanding of the value of his class for her son, the woman saw him in a field with his sheep. The elderly teacher walked over to the car, put his hand on the door, and spoke very slowly, "If I should live a thousand years, I should not receive a letter as nice as the one I received from you."

Another teacher expressed thanks for a letter saying, "I put all my good letters in a box to read when I retire. When I am old and question what good I ever did in all the years of teaching teenagers, I plan to take the box out and read the letters again. Thank you very much. That is where your letter is."

It is difficult to describe the priceless value of a sincere letter of thanks.

Alison
Buchanan
1999

More Quiet Gestures

Learn Names

The Words "I'm Sorry"

Pass Along Hobbies

Return Postcards

Traveling Parents

Penny Potential

Offer Laughter

Dress in Bright Colors

Empty the Dishwasher

Favorite Music

Thank You

Surprise an Old Committee

Complete Directions

A Dozen Plus Reflections

Learn Names

---

*L*earn names. Everyone everywhere loves to be called by name. Acknowledging a person specifically is acknowledging a unique persona. And a name sprinkled freely within conversation is a polite and friendly form of recognition.

Unfortunately, remembering names is a failure of mine, but soon my age will offer me the excuse of expected lapses in memory. My husband, however, receives an A++. He even remembers the first, middle, and last names of his teachers in grade school. I can only imagine that his parents and teachers must have stressed the exciting sounds of names and the importance of remembering every one at an early age.

It's a generous habit. Use names; it gives everyone a good feeling on an ordinary day, and indicates, "Someone knows me and knows me by name."

The Words, "I'm Sorry"

When someone has had a great loss or experienced an extreme illness in the family, acknowledging the problem means everything. Some friends think that avoiding the subject is the kindest gesture, but that is usually not true. Hearing, "I'm sorry," or "I am sad for your loss," means a lot.

People feel awkward mentioning another's seemingly endless difficulty or approaching the subject of grief, but by speaking up in a gentle way, we acknowledge the devastation and loneliness felt in another's heart. They have the choice whether to respond with details of the experience or merely to answer "Thank you" and move on to the next topic of conversation.

When you say, "I am sorry for your sadness," they will appreciate your sincere gesture of soft words.

Pass Along Hobbies

---

*T*each a child, a grand-child, or a friend your hobby, whether it's needle-work, woodworking, painting, building models, playing an instrument, bird watching or enjoying photography. All wonder-filled hobbies can be loved by another. It is easy to question whether or not someone else would like what we like, but you may be surprised at another's response to learn something new. Enthusiasm is contagious.

To pass along your passion is to pass along a part of yourself. It might take patience, precious time, and also some money, but you will be offering a new pleasure for others to enjoy for a lifetime. Sharing your talent is real generosity.

Return Postcards

When cleaning out papers from an attic, basement, file, or desk drawer, make the extra effort to send the special notes and pictures onward. Returning them to the original writers or relatives re-awakens the past. Instantly, the mind's eye gets busy recalling details of a day, an event, or a vacation. Receiving old postcards, letters, photos, and holiday cards is like having a carrier pigeon deliver poignant moments from years gone by. They carry the message, "Someone is still thinking of you."

When I received a letter recently, with old photos from an elderly woman, it did seem like another piece of regular mail. Then I began to replay in my mind the steps she had taken to send the package. It contained pictures that she knew I would like, shot decades earlier of my parents and their friends. She had to find my address, buy a mailing envelope, weigh it, stamp it, and traipse to a post office. The process absorbed a lot of her time just to please me, and it did, greatly!

Let's admit it. Returning paper treasures adds more chores to daily routines. But the effort offers serendipitous generosity and re-awakens life's timeline for others.

Traveling Parents

Praise Moms and Dads traveling on trains and planes with small children and give special admiration to the little ones who are happy with distractions. Parents appreciate generous compliments about their children's good behavior. They have probably been holding their breath the whole trip hoping that the moments of calm will not burst into chaos, which could happen, because children are children. And, remember, good behavior just doesn't happen; it is a growing work of art.

Penny Potential

At church, a giant jar almost filled with pennies piqued my curiosity and I wondered where the money would go when it reached the brim. Someone there explained that it was a project for the children to help less fortunate children. In a few weeks when the jug was full, the young would vote for one favorite cause from a list of several, and a check would be sent to help other young people. They named the jar, "Pennies from Heaven."

At home, a similar jar for pennies could be placed in a hallway, on the kitchen counter, or by the back door for family members to participate. Everyone could get in the habit of emptying pockets of pennies into the jar. The money mound would slowly grow. Then the family could agree on a way to reach out to others. Call it "Penny Potential."

Offer Laughter

When folks are unable to leave their home, take the world to them. Drop in on a friend and bring some item for "Show and Tell and Remember." We have many things tucked in our homes that could encourage laughter and offer topics for conversation beyond the usual weather, health, diet, and medications. It could be cartoons from an old magazine, photos or used postcards, a pair of white gloves, a darning egg, costumes from the costume box or hats from the closet. Funny items can enliven conversations and spark humor with people who are housebound. It's healthy and lifts the curtain of sameness.

Dress in Bright Colors

What we wear can affect our spirit for the day and influence others. Clothes can brighten or subdue a mood. This is why a volunteer sometimes wears a different colored sneaker on each foot or varied colored laces on her shoes. They are guaranteed to produce happy reactions from the patients at the hospital where she works.

At a senior residence home, a fellow often wears a shocking pink, very handsome, cable knit sweater as he moves about during the day. It cheers everyone and automatically brings smiles to those around him. He is not overlooked. He is noticed in pink, a gift from someone who loves him.

Dressing in bright colors can affect a happy mood for others.

Empty the Dishwasher

Without a suggestion or a request, surprise a mom or the usual kitchen worker and empty the dishwasher. Family members or guests are prized when they step forward to help in this way. It is the one time that opening an empty box is pure joy. Emptying the garbage or wiping the kitchen counters are the only rivals for most disliked duties in the kitchen. Feel free to do any tasks. Your snapshot of goodness will bring great delight.

Favorite Music

When an older friend became ill, people were discouraged from sending books, plants, and other gifts. But, when pressed, his wife would add a little idea, "Remember, Mike loves gospel music." Mike received a lot of music, and his family took it to his hospital room with a simple player to help pass the hours.

Classical, country, piano, folk, jazz, or quiet rock may be another person's choice while resting or dozing off to sleep. Bring a friend's favorite music from a home collection or try something new in the same genre. Listening quietly may add pleasurable moments during recuperation.

Thank You

Say thank you to people you seldom think to thank: the people around you who do things that you don't want to do. Some workers go 365 days between holidays without much ado or many moments of thank you. Consider that if you haven't been showing appreciation, more than likely, no one else has been doing so either. Simple words like, "Thanks. Really, thank you for doing that today. I appreciate it," make another person feel very good.

If you think nice things, say them. Generous thoughts don't need to be stored away for the future. If you don't voice them now, they may never be said.

Surprise an
Old Committee

*B*ring an element of
surprise and pleasure by gathering a committee
from years past that once worked diligently on a
town project, an auction, or a school function. Such
a gathering continues a sense of appreciation of past
contributions.

Often when an important commitment ends,
everyone vows to continue friendships. Then daily
lives fill and new obligations get in the way. Years
gradually pass and the idea is forgotten. We move
off the stage and separately recall the happy times
spent together.

Invite past groups or perhaps the older members of an organization who share an interest.
Everyone will remember the days of involvement
and leadership and will enjoy discussing how things
have changed. It will be an active gathering and a
generous gesture.

Complete Directions

———————

"Are you a local?" came the voice from a car window. I was a bit confused whether the man meant, did I know my way around the town or, rather, around the large care center, since I was standing in its parking lot at the time.

"Yes," I ventured, assuming that I would soon learn why he needed a "local." He was very lost and miles from the right road to take to his destination.

Our exchange took quite some time to set him straight. Sometimes it takes many minutes to give clear and accurate directions, but it helps a stranger who was probably reluctant to ask in the first place.

A Dozen Plus Reflections

S omeone placed more than one dozen fresh arrangements of red, white, and blue flowers in a large road-stop restroom, and, with the reflection in the mirrors, it multiplied the beauty. Overwhelmed by this abundant display, a camera was quickly found to capture the patriotic statement.

There must have been a story to encourage such a compelling expression in a public place. Unfortunately no one was nearby to thank and to hear the admiration for the spirit of the flowers. But the sight was unforgettable, and no doubt brought equal surprise and pleasure to all others who entered the room. What a special gesture!

Of Mind and Spirit

Listen and Ask
Write Your Story
Give Slack
Hello Hello
Praise the Servers
Friendly Question
First Birthday
Letter to the Very Ill
Tribute Wish
Shiny Trophy
For Confidence
Twenty-One Positives
Peace
Generosity to Yourself

Listen and Ask

---

*I*f you feel concerned about what you hear behind someone's words on the phone, ask the simple question, "Are you all right?" Those four words carry so much heart. They acknowledge that you have heard pain or predicament. Your words reflect the feeling that you would like to know more.

Four very special words, "Are you all right?"

Write Your Story

Writing an autobiography offers the author the gift of reflection and the opportunity to share memories with following generations.

Over the years a woman has written about her forty-eight years of married life in poetry form: the birthdays, graduations, anniversaries, births, deaths, vacations, and celebrations. Recently she had the collection printed for family and friends; it is a prized possession. The poems are filled with descriptions and emotional reactions to every major happening; now future generations will have the chance to know the family very well.

Another autobiography is being written in prose. It will not be strictly chronological. Instead, the writer has been sketching memories of significant events, interesting times, and special traditions whenever they spring into her thoughts. During this process she has realized how serene her earlier life had been, and her stories tell of the quiet, simple pleasures. Someday relatives will enjoy her written reflections, penned in a spiral notebook, without a computer. Perhaps the concluding line will be, "In my world we were used to serenity."

It's generosity to take the time to write your story.

Give Slack

*I*f the silver is tarnished, it may be from the water they have; if a sink is filled with dishes, their priority may be on family, not appearance that day; or if a house looks topsy-turvy, it may be a place of creativity. Hold judgment. There may be good reasons for situations that we do not like at first glance. Try to understand or imagine excuses. So many of our homes could use a sign to move day by day from room to room. "Work in Progress. You'll like the final product."

Hello Hello

"*H*ello Hello. How far are you going?"

The conductor repeated this greeting to each passenger as she moved down the aisle on the train. Everyone could hear the tune. "Hello Hello. Hello Hello." There was a friendly song to it, and, as her voice approached, I did hope that she would greet me, too, with her musical words. She was sweeping through the railroad car with cheer.

We had a short conversation and she clipped my ticket. I wish I knew her name. As she continued on to the next passenger with her effective greeting, I wondered what color she would paint her railroad car if she were given a paint-box. It would probably be bright, maybe sunshine yellow. "Hello Hello."

Praise the Servers

s four servers bustled about a large party, concerned that everyone have drinks, hors d'oeuvres, omelets, and light fare, a conversation stopped me. The daughter of the hostess was speaking to one of the servers. "Thank you so much. Everything is delicious. We're having a wonderful time at our own party because of you. You are making it nice for us all. Thank you."

His reply: "It's our job, but I wish more people would say that to us. They don't. They just want us to serve and get out of the way. What you said means a lot. I'll tell the other waiters. Thank you."

Even when people are just "doing their job," they appreciate praise.

Friendly Question

At 4:00 one afternoon we were in a big hurry. The car always liked to travel too fast along a familiar stretch of road. We'd memorized the speed limit, but this time our minds were focused on our destination. We were talking plane tickets, money, equipment, et cetera, when the red and blue lights started flashing from the car behind us.

Instantly we knew that we were wrong by seventeen miles an hour. The policeman approached our car. "You know, you folks were speeding. Is there any reason why you were going so fast?" What an amazing and generous question! The policeman cared. We explained our predicament: We're going to the airport to catch a plane, and we had a late start from home.

After returning from our trip, we told the police commissioner in town how much we appreciated the polite question. "Is there any reason why you were going so fast?"

First Birthday

A bear, a dozen roses, a card. One, two, three gifts were delivered to a young family from godparents. A furry bear was given to celebrate the baby's first birthday, a dozen roses were sent for the mother and dad, but the card, the third present, touched them the most. Even when the mom called to read it to her mother-in-law, they both cried! The words on the card conveyed so much love and understanding of new parenthood. "May God bless her parents."

Letter to the Very Ill

Write friends and relatives who are very ill and tell them how much they mean to you. Fill the lines with moments you shared that affected your life, the ones that were special or funny or gave you new direction.

Of course, you could wait and write the relatives of those who have passed on, recounting to them stories of times together. But isn't it better for the special people themselves to know how grateful you are to have been on the same path in this life? You should tell them so.

As health starts to wane, many people begin to wonder about the significance of their time on earth. They may ask, "Did I do a good job with this life?" That's why it's important to send a personal letter to affirm the wonderful value of your relationship. The letter will be a resounding "Thank you. Thank you. You touched my life in so many ways and made it better. Please know I will remember."

Tribute Wish

A gentleman's final wishes were expressed in his obituary. He requested the following: Don't bother to come to my funeral. Instead, take a walk in our favorite woods, go fishing with a child, visit another elderly pal, call a relative and chat, or just do something for others. Giving an afternoon of kindness to yourself or someone else would be the best tribute to me.

Writing his final thoughts, the gentleman was obviously thinking of others. Was this how he had spent his days on earth, other-directed? His obituary was different, and it gave his friends and scores of readers food for thought. Perhaps he was creating a continuum of generosity as he passed from life to life eternal.

Shiny Trophy

*I*n the excitement of winning the game, a teenager gave his trophy to his girlfriend of the moment. Most trophies were engraved cups or butter plates, but this little one had design and could sit on a dresser or bric-a-brac shelf very easily. It was shaped like a miniature soup tureen with handles and was engraved on the lid.

Forty-five years later the family wondered what had become of the trophy and remarked that it would have been nice if she had returned it. "Absolutely not!" was the instant reply of the now grown teenager. "I've learned that she has had a hard life, and I'm glad she has it."

His response carried the spirit of compassion for her difficulties and the hope that the little bit of silver brings her good memories of times years ago.

For Confidence

*L*eave a message for someone close to you who has an important meeting, a presentation, or an interview soon. A familiar voice that offers encouragement and interest carries power. An answering machine is a perfect medium. The message can be played again and again before he or she leaves to conquer the appointment.

"Tomorrow, may the winds of knowledge surround you. May the breeze carry confidence to you. Plant your feet, lift the room with your smile and open your thoughts to all you have learned. You are prepared. Enjoy the moment."

Sometimes generosity is simply a thoughtful message or a quick phone call.

Twenty-One Positives

Children may wonder what their parents really think of them; a positive list given on a special occasion is a perfect way to let them know.

When a daughter was approaching her twenty-first birthday, her mother decided to give her a list of twenty-one beautiful things she loved about her. The mother praised her personality traits, confidence in tackling disappointments, enthusiasm for new opportunities, significant accomplishments to be proud of and much more. She also elaborated on certain memories.

Composing the list was a precious exercise and required much reflection. Daily the mother had always said, "Love you," but now her daughter knew twenty-one reasons why.

Peace

Aheartwarming aftermath of the September 11, 2001 disasters was the kindness and generosity extended by friends, family, workers, and strangers to one another. For months the world turned extremely kind. Even today, just mentioning the words, *Nine-Eleven,* changes facades. Instantly people feel a sense of commonality and begin to share their experiences. Compassion draws them closer for the moment, and life pauses briefly for the compelling exchange. Stillness enters. Then peace-filled wishes are expressed again, and the people part. It's generous communication.

Generosity to Yourself

Grant yourself moments of generosity. Daily we check off hours of obligations to others and we seldom reflect on small touches of time we give to ourselves.

Your own time can be slipped in between busy schedules. It's like the space on a wall around numerous works of art. It is necessary and allows focus and anticipation to flow. Daily lives are so crammed there is hardly a millimeter for space between pictures, but we need the extra space. It's our free moment!

The popularity of spas, coffee shops, and yoga classes indicates that people are trying to find ways to rejuvenate. Be generous to yourself. Find stillness in public places or alone places. Take a class or, for just a moment, write a few lines in a journal, sketch a picture, play an instrument, or doodle on a notepad and daydream. Even fifteen minutes of sitting or reading or walking outside can replenish the soul and refill your cup of life with peace and quiet.

Earth Connections

Plant Together

Plant a tree with someone young. Plant it on Arbor Day, Earth Day, a birthday, or any day. Quickly take a snapshot to record how you both looked with the tree at its beginning. Then, as a team, water and care for it, watch it grow, and when it is large enough, hang a birdhouse from a branch to offer a home to a woodland creature. Together you will have made an earth connection and added beauty to a landscape.

Someone Else's Daffodils

One afternoon years ago, a little boy snapped off a handful of flowers from a hillside on a neighbor's property. He was on his way home from the bus stop, when he spotted a field full of yellow daffodils growing in clumps in the grass, and must have felt a calling to collect a bouquet.

When the kind neighbor saw his busy hands attacking her daffodils, she came out to inquire about his activity. He innocently explained, "Oh, these are for my mother!" How could she answer anything but, "That's very nice. I know she will love them." Then the understanding neighbor watched him diligently gather more for his bouquet, realizing that the only boundary he knew was a large heart of spring love for his mom.

Move the Bug

Carry the wasp safely outside in a cup. Move the little, black, jumping spider to a plant. Find an appropriate leaf for the crawling bug. That's just what happens at a friend's house. She observes small critters and moves them to better habitats when they are lost. Saving them is her quiet way of preserving nature's diversity and giving earth's creatures a bit more longevity.

Taking Pumpkins

Over time we had several ministers come and go at our church. Not one knew our names. Coming and going we exchanged pleasantries, smiles, and handshakes, but no names. When a new minister arrived one September, I decided that he was going to know our family. We would give him a gift.

My children were very little at the time and into the spirit of Halloween. In October we selected a pumpkin and carried it to his office with a card that included all our names. The minister appeared delighted. It became a yearly ritual. I am happy to add that the minister always wrote the children a personal thank you note and he always knew their names. With gladness, this gift of earth's bounty harvested a special people connection.

Have Tools, Will Dig

"*D*esire to work in a garden this summer. Will plant, weed, water and maintain. Can design area. Only ask payment for plant material. Call after 6:00 P.M."

This offer was placed in the classified section of a newspaper by a twenty-six year old who lived in an apartment and missed her garden. She hoped a shut-in or senior might respond to the advertisement with eagerness to have a garden again.

It's a generous concept to make a garden for someone else.

A Live Memorial

Sixteen acres of original native prairie were given to a Land Trust and dedicated as a memorial to a loving mother and wife who had grown up on the grasslands of Kansas. The farm had been in her husband's family for three generations, since 1895, and the land stretched so far "you could see beyond the day after tomorrow." The horizon had no end. It was a place where buffalo roamed, Native Americans lived, pioneers passed by, and then farmers came to settle.

The sixteen acres have always remained prime prairie. The soil has never been plowed. The family has tended it properly. It is mowed and baled yearly and periodically burned for renewal so no trees can grow. Over two hundred species of wildflowers and native grasses have been identified on this sweet, precious patch of prairie that flourishes with insects, birds and wildlife. Once a year it is opened for a Prairie Walk offered with an ecologist. Otherwise, the land rests and grows and blows and stays the same. Setting aside this grassland in the Kansas Land Trust means the cycle of life will continue there unaltered. What a beautiful gift to preserve nature on a piece of protected prairie!

Touch of Nature

When a gardening group gathers for its monthly meeting, every member brings a token gift from her yard to contribute to an arrangement: a flower or two in bloom, buds on a stem, seed pods, or a branch of green from a shrub or tree. The collected material is placed artistically in a glass container or a covered can to become a "Get Well" gift for an ill member. It's delivered right after the meeting along with a card signed by many.

If every member is healthy, the vase becomes a "Congratulations Vase" for a successful project, a "Good Wish Vase" or even an "Encouragement Vase" for someone who is about to put on an event. The small tokens of nature arranged by friends personalize the bouquet and give a special touch of kindness.

The Boy's Gift

A boy and his dad loved to hike the hills. They watched for changes in the seasons and birds migrating through the territory. They liked the rock formations, and the peaceful river that ran through the land. It was their weekend habit to visit this natural world many miles beyond the road.

Then word spread that the park was going to be sold to developers. Houses, strip-malls, river restaurants, and billboards were all mentioned in conversations. The boy and his dad were horror struck. What to do?

The eleven-year-old reached out to his friends. He asked for no presents for his birthday, only gifts of money to protect the open space. They responded. His total donation of almost $200 was given with a personal commitment. "You can count on me for another donation next year, but I hope the area will have been saved by then." Perhaps his example will make an impression on others who will join in a worthy cause.

A Life Tree

When stumped about what to give a friend for his birthday, the answer came in the form of Mother Nature's pruning. After a storm, we found a broken branch to use as a small tree for hanging photos of his life from its limbs. We cemented it in a pot, tied on the pictures and the result was a personal gift. The gentleman liked his life tree so much it stood in the corner of his study for several years.

Remember Me

Perhaps it is a generous moment to stop and express sorrow at the passing of an endangered species. When I learned that the Ivory-Billed Woodpecker was now considered extinct, I expressed my sadness at the loss in the following free verse:

We were seen through binoculars, painted, and photographed. Created awe with our extensive white on wings, whether folded or in flight. And tip-to-tip our wings spanned three to four feet. Extraordinary!

Were we homeless . . . our forest deforested? Without food? The water polluted? Perhaps pesticides? The land being timbered for buildings, roads, parking lots?

Why our unique structure? Our singular DNA? Our special contribution to the woodland?

No beauty, no flutter, no breath . . . just a quiet disappearance. My airborne colors, red, black, and white, now feather the earth.

Remember me.

One more beautiful species gone.

Did anyone notice? Does anyone care?

Sunlight

*L*et's acknowledge the sun's ordinary goodness and greet the morning light with thank you.

After days of the drearies, drizzles, and drabs, yellow from sky's prism appears. Sunlight suddenly hugs the earth at early dawn and smiles upon the windows in our homes. It tickles our senses. "Wake up. It's going to be a good day!"

Become Outsiders Again

A horticulturist/photographer studied one piece of his property where trees had fallen across a stream and wildflowers grew. He photographed birds, plants, animals, changing shadows, everything that altered the scene at different hours, in different seasons. Then he gave a stirring lecture on observation using this one small spot as his example. All the action opened our eyes. Nature never stops!

In recent years, the skill of observing the outside world has faded. Days are spent comfortably inside: in cars and malls, near television sets, or on computers. Now we watch through our windows and adjust the thermostat. After centuries of being farmers, we are Insiders.

"Go out and play." "Get out of the house." "Go find something to do outside." These were some of a mother's favorite words years ago. The idea was to go outside into the fresh air, play, and get some exercise. Inevitably, as children, we enjoyed the surprises in nature: bugs, rabbits, snowflakes, leaves changing, and the odd rock here and there. We looked about from ground to sky. We were observing!

As adults, we can regain the art of observation we had as a child. What we see and know and love in the out-of-doors, we will save.

Missy's Minute

*I*n the closing minute of every club meeting for two years, the president gave a quick exhortation for our planet. It was "Missy's Minute" for conservation. As a persuasive power of one, she alerted the one hundred and fifty members monthly to act and pass on knowledge to their children, neighbors, friends, and public officials. She hoped for a chain reaction of caring for the earth. Missy's Minute was packed with facts and written with considerable thought. "More awareness—more action" became the club's conservation motto.

Our greatest generosity to the earth is good stewardship. Around the world environmental leaders stress that if we exercise restraint today, we will help ensure natural resources and biodiversity for centuries to come. Motivation to save the earth is found in many places: written publications, popular songs, powerful environmental television and movie presentations, on products and bumper stickers, and sometimes in a moment's inspirational talk called "Missy's Minute."

A Missy's Minute Excerpt

———

Afew words from one of Missy's Minutes capture the essence of our earth connection:

> Please consider, from time to time, those places that offer you solace, serenity, and renewal; those places that touch your souls in times of trouble or crisis: the mountains, the deserts, the forests, oceans, lakes and rivers. These are the places that make you remember who you are, what you believe in, what you cherish, and what makes you complete.

Gestures from Times Past

Tip of the Hat

May Basket

Simple Stockings

Sundays

Holding Doors and Pulling out Chairs

Invitations with RSVP

Decoration Day

Knowing Neighbors

24-Hour Deadline

A Song and a Smile

Saving History

The Pearl Necklace

Tip of the Hat

In the days of my Dad, a gentleman tipped his hat when he greeted a woman. That gesture gave a quiet sense of acknowledgement that meant, "You are special. I tip my hat." It's a vision I keep of my Dad, a gentleman.

If wearing hats came back into fashion, would this generous gesture of respect, tipping a hat, also return?

May Basket

At the beginning of May, mothers would fill small baskets with flowers and candies. Then the little children would run up and put them on the porches of friends and neighbors for a springtime surprise. No card was included. It was a guessing moment. Who brought the May basket?

How personal! We could create springtime baskets, too. So many people would love our floral surprises: some rocks, moss, ivy, twigs with buds, a few flowers, and candies tucked in a basket. The greatest gift would be that it was grown and arranged at home. Simple generosity.

Simple Stockings

*D*ecades ago, Christmas stockings were very simple. As children, our stockings were mother's old nylons. They were dandy because they were long and stretchy. We could see what we were getting all the way down to the toe, where there was always a tangerine or orange because fruit was a tradition from even earlier times.

I wish Santa Claus had kept a list of everything that he had put into the stockings just one December 24 when I was very young. That would be a special gift to read today.

Sundays

Sundays were family days. Families usually ate a leisurely Sunday dinner sitting around the dining room table and talking with relatives. The pace was slower. Sometimes, after church, they communed with nature and would take a walk in the woods, or sometimes they would take the automobile for a drive in the countryside. Then in the evening, the family played cards and games together. It was a time for people to write their weekly letters home to parents who lived elsewhere. Family togetherness was the goal on Sundays.

How could we retrieve these moments in our present day, fast-changing time? Turn off the phones, the computers, and the televisions, slow the fast meals down, postpone the trip to buy more things and set aside general obligations. Could simplicity and togetherness return for a day? It happens in northern climes when a big snowstorm keeps us housebound, and there is a sensation that the elements are carrying us backward to a quiet time.

Holding Doors, Pulling out Chairs

*T*here has been a recent revival of young men holding doors, pulling out chairs for women, and later helping them with their coats. These considerate acts have pleased ladies in the past and offer graciousness for the future.

Because my definition of generosity includes gestures of thoughtful manners, this short chapter on old-fashioned gentlemanliness is appropriate. Like diamonds, good manners shine.

Invitations with RSVP

As was done in the olden days, RSVP printed on an invitation meant respond immediately and the recipients of invitations did just that. They didn't put it in a pile to consider a month hence or to wait until the last minute to see if a better party or opportunity might arrive. Years ago the invited appreciated being included on the guest list and knew the host or hostess needed to know how many friends would attend the event. RSVP meant respond and people responded.

An invitation is a hostess's generosity; your timely reply is generosity in return.

Decoration Day

*T*oday we call it Memorial Day, but in the early 1900s it was called Decoration Day. The last Monday in May was a day set aside to decorate the graves of veterans and family members. Everyone went to the town cemeteries to tidy the monuments, to plant flowers and place flags for the servicemen.

Life is continuity. Are we setting good examples for the younger generations today? Most cemeteries need our attention and family burial places deserve our respect.

Knowing Neighbors

Generations ago, people didn't move frequently so they really knew all the folks in the neighborhood. But, when a new neighbor did move in, everyone brought fresh produce and baked goods as welcome gifts. Neighbors relied on one another, shared life's ups and downs, and made home projects central topics for conversation. Regularly, folks helped one another with chores and when trouble visited, they knew immediately who to call for help: their reliable friends, their neighbors. The interdependence gave much needed support and marked a strong community.

Aspects of days gone by make us ponder the changes today in towns and cities stressed by growing populations. Neighborhoods once gave identity and connection and exemplified generosity in good times and bad. Can we help bring back a strong sense of caring for neighbors as a normal part of everyday life? 'Twould be great!

24-Hour Deadline

When one professor at college said that a paper was due on October 25, he meant any minute day or night on the twenty-fifth. His tradition was to open his house that evening for students to bring their work and come for a class supper. If the party had ended, you could place the paper in his mailbox by midnight. It was a personal way to soften the blow of a big assignment. He also knew that students procrastinated and midnight would be a friendly extension of several hours.

Today with computers, this unique touch by a professor probably wouldn't happen, but we were grateful in 1956 for the additional time. I have only a few exact memories of college, but I can remember precisely the professor's name, the course, his house and mailbox, and the hour I turned my paper in!

A Song and a Smile

*T*he cat's tail moved back and forth and its eyes moved left and right on the clock. The little patient just sat with his feet dangling over the side of the examining table. Time slowly ticking by on the cat on the wall. This was the scary time.

Then quietly, a voice began to sing down the hall. "Oh, Danny boy, the pipes, the pipes are calling, From glen to glen, and down the mountain side . . ." or maybe, another favorite, "I'll take you home again, Kathleen, across the ocean wild and wide . . ."

Every child and parent knew the doctor was moving down the hall. The melody soothed nerves, we knew our turn was next, and then there he was at our door. His song and smile and a lollipop in his hand carried kindness and were gifts to his patients for the thirty-one years he practiced pediatrics in our town.

Saving History

No one wanted to use it, no one knew what to do with it, but no one wanted it destroyed. "It" was a beautiful, historic church built circa 1850 with a lonely sign tacked to the door: "For Sale . . . $1.00 . . . if you will move it."

Older structures reveal the history of an earlier time. Their buyers give townspeople and visitors the generous gift of antique, different, unique, and often beautiful dwellings. Caring for historic landmarks is a challenge. They are more costly to maintain and renovate than more modern places, and there are often restrictions on alterations. But the effort helps protect the historic character of an area. Towns and cities are more interesting with examples of past and present side by side on the same street.

Let's express thanks to historical societies and owners of historic and special plaque buildings (dating at least one hundred years earlier). Preserving old houses is great generosity. It saves the architectural beauty of the past for the future.

Pearl Necklace

*I*n the 1920s, they were dancing the Charleston at a college ball when her pearl necklace broke and the white gems spread over the dance floor. The young man scurried to gather them up and placed them in his pocket.

The blind date continued into the evening and the young man's heart was smitten. He returned to his college with a pocketful of pearls and planned the next step of courtship in the form of letters. He enclosed one pearl with each note, slowly returning her necklace. After mailing the last pearl, the young man offered his heart and asked her to marry him.

The necklace was restrung, probably a few pearls short, and the couple was happily married for forty-six years, until death took his sweetheart away. Now the necklace is a priceless possession of their daughter's.

Generosity Is . . .

Generosity Is

*b*eing invited into a younger relative's world: a scientific laboratory, naval station, archeological dig, or wherever his or her time and energy and thought are focused. It's a treat for a relative to visit for even a moment, an hour, or a day.

*S*uddenly flying to spend a weekend with a friend who anxiously awaits news from medical tests. Being alone is difficult; being with a friend makes the waiting time go faster. "I'm coming" puts air back into a balloon.

Generosity Is

*R*esponding to holiday cards in wintertime. In the year's busiest month, we receive long notes, some sad, many excited, and instantly tuck them in a basket to answer later. Many await our reply. Acknowledging all the news is a kind gesture and might advance a New Year's resolution to do better with letter writing.

One friend's method is to place each card alphabetically in a file. When she writes the next year's Christmas cards, she rereads the old card and answers it then. Thus, they all get answered in a timely, organized fashion. (This friend also has on file every single card she and her husband have received. It's a mighty collection that she can share with the families if ever they wish to see their cards again.)

Generosity Is

———

*S*haring plants from a garden. It hurts gardeners to put plants into their own compost or to sell their home to a non-gardener, knowing that perhaps, away will go the ferns and roses, lilies and peonies. Instead, give your flowers and shrubs away with flourish. A gardener's joy is meeting his or her favorite plants again in a friend's yard.

*h*elping a young person get his or her first job after college. It's like having someone hold your foot, so you can swing into the saddle on the horse. Once up, you're on your own. But getting the toe into the stirrup is a tremendous boost.

*t*he gift of *FORGIVENESS*.

Generosity Is

*i*nviting members of a congregation to sing in the choir at the services in summertime. Many who sit weekly in the pews secretly desire to sing, but question the true choir-quality of their voices. This is their chance. One music director even publishes the titles of the summer hymns in early June to show how familiar the songs will be and to offer encouragement to join. There are no rehearsals and all feel most welcome.

*h*anging an arrangement of field flowers in a straw hat on the front door to welcome friends on moving-in day. "Welcome to the west side of town. You'll like it here. We're closer to the sunsets."

*u*sing colorful washcloths as napkins instead of using paper ones. They feel good, stay on laps, are easy to launder, and it's a small step to save our forests.

Generosity Is

_K_eeping the soft animals with names like Donkey Doodle, Beary, and George, and the Blankies of childhood safely in a box to bring back memories and sighs of "Oh my!" in later years. Children usually have only one super-duper comfort piece, and it's kind to let it survive no matter what its condition.

_S_aying, "Yes, I'll do it," after a committee chair presents a situation and asks for a volunteer to do the job. Hearing "Yes" is a day's best gift to a leader. "Yes" answers prayers every day.

_M_aking another's older retirement years more comfortable.

Generosity Is

*C*reating an award, a scholarship or a lecture series in memory of someone loved very much by you. The on-going gift that touches and inspires others will glow as a remembrance of a vital, exceptional friend or family member.

*C*omposing a piece on the piano to express joy for someone who is completing medical treatments. Composing music for another is the creative expression of an inner spirit, and the notes are personal. They are chosen with care to carry a heart in the sound.

Generosity Is

———

*t*raveling to pick up an adult child who has had an accident or whose heart has been broken. It is a time when he or she needs the comfort of a parent and a home. Fathers often answer this call for love in a kind and patient way that is always remembered.

*t*aking household items, toys, and clothes that you no longer want or need to a thrift shop, donation shelter, or church treasure sale, instead of throwing them into a town dump or rented dumpster to be wasted forever. The time and effort required to pass along usables from rugs to teaspoons to hammers and nails is real generosity for others.

*n*ot taking things for granted. It is remembering and expressing gratitude for the little and the big things and the things that are always "just there."

Generosity Is

Working at an agency that helps needy children. In late summer at one social service, families are invited to come choose new clothes, shoes, and supplies for school. Sometimes the helpers receive thank you notes. One card read: When I got home, I put my clothes on my bed and just looked at them and cried. Thank you for my new clothes. Others have sent drawings of themselves in their new clothes, and one little boy waved his new things out of the bus window, shouting with glee, "I have new clothes! I have new clothes!" Just imagine!

Generosity Is

_b_eing the kind and patient hairdresser who brings joy to older ladies and gents week after week at the beauty parlor or barber shop. Many of the elderly have general infirmities and probably give small gratuities, but this never affects the close relationship built over years. The appointments always offer moments of personal attention and beauty and friendly faces with familiar chatter. Watch them. Hair specialists and barbers offer a very special brand of kindness.

Generosity Is

*f*orgetting a wallet and having the restaurant manager give the teenager forty dollars from his own pocket. "Pay for your meal, then take your date on rides at the entertainment park. When you can, send me a check and help someone else when you have the chance." The time was World War II and forty dollars was equivalent to over one hundred dollars today. Imagine the generosity and the trust! (Since that time he has helped another fellow in a lost-wallet predicament. After paying for the stranger's meal, he charged him only a promise to do the same someday, somewhere for someone else.)

Generosity Is

---

*M*aking use of the surge of energy felt upon hearing news of the birth of a child in your family. Creativity often swells to new heights in the excitement. Paint, write, compose, sculpture; express the joy! It will be a perfect personal present for the baby a bit later. People have been inspired to write books and songs and one man went to his art studio and was drawn to paint a life-size portrait of what his brand-new baby daughter would look like at age twenty-five. She's beautiful on canvas, and she's grown up to match the painting in real life.

*g*athering grandchildren for a specific event or trip. During summer vacation one grandmother invited eight granddaughters between the ages of nine and twelve to visit her and attend needlepoint camp. Together they sewed and swam and went sightseeing for a week. What a gift from a grand-mother age ninety!

Generosity Is

----

*b*aking a cake for the second grade classroom party to please her child. When the teacher asked for someone to provide the dessert, eager to participate, a little boy spoke up, "Oh, my mother will do it. The kitchen is her natural habitat!" This was a kind challenge for a mom who wasn't truly "at home" in the kitchen and who didn't know much about baking.

*r*aising your hand at a charity auction to raise the bid, not because you wanted or needed the item, but because you knew the children at the school needed a new playground.

*O*ffering to pay for books each semester for a college student who carries a heavy class schedule while working long hours at extra jobs to pay for an education. This specific gift gives support to a young person who is determined to receive a college degree. There are only twenty-four hours in a day for students, too!

Generosity Is

---

*b*eing a shopkeeper who shares his community spirit by providing window space for displays
of upcoming town events, bulletin board space for
important notices and poster space for happenings
of town-wide interest. Many shopkeepers quietly
give generous support in myriad ways every day to
their communities.

*C*hoosing a career that protects, aids, and
offers other people security. Many volunteer, many
are paid, but either way, the jobs place them in peril
to make other people's lives safer. There are too
many occuptions with this description to list here,
but you know them. Please thank these dedicated
workers whenever and however you can. This para-
graph reminds me of a bumper sticker I saw years
ago that has given me many moments of thought: If
you like your freedom, thank a veteran.

Generosity Is

───────

*t*reating friends and families to holiday affairs year after year, in spite of the hosts' periodic desire to adjust the tradition. Guests usually love the gatherings the way they have always been. They desire no changes: same food, same place, same date and time, same people, and same entertainment. To please, the hosts kindly move their calendars about so that the annual Easter Egg Hunts, baseball games, family Fourth of July picnics, and one Thanksgiving football game continuous since 1942 can happen on schedule. Thank you to the tradition-makers.

*p*assing along a compliment heard about someone. Nice thoughts carried back will always make that special or talented person feel good.

Generosity is being magnanimous in any simple, personal, or extra-special way.

Holidays and
Celebrations

Floating Candles

Swapping Charities

Handmade Presents

Bride's Dress

Everyone's Invited

Cousin Connection

Birthdays

Occasion for a Toast

Valentine's Day

Halloween Photos

Sweet Surprise

Engraving Traditions

Floating Candles

*D*oing the unusual for a celebration can create generosity to remember.

For my parents' fiftieth wedding anniversary, we took our young children to their grandparents' pond and floated candles at dusk as a surprise. We had painted fifty small square platforms and placed the candles in drilled holes. The grandchildren were excited with their gift of lights as we pushed them off from the shore. The fountain in the middle made ripples to carry the small islands of light, and the two white swans, Romeo and Juliet, glided between them. The scene is still a vivid memory for all.

Swapping Charities

A family with members aged fourteen to eighty-four had a challenge to find the right presents to give one another at holiday time. A teenager came up with the perfect solution: swap charities, not store-bought gifts.

Now, everyone arrives at the dinner with a card revealing the name and address of his or her favorite charity. All cards go into a bowl. One relative at a time picks a card, then the nominee tells about the need and why a gift of money would be meaningful. Afterward, each person decides how much to give and sends a check to the good cause.

The simplicity is appealing. All ages participate. No hassle, no wrapping, no last minute shopping, and throughout the year, the family members can discuss charities with one another. The gifts create interaction between generations and are filled with the spirit of giving.

Handmade Presents

---

*H*andmade gifts and homemade cooking treats are among the best presents we can receive. They are priceless generosity because of the hours, days, and sometimes weeks of labor spent designing and completing them. It is wonderful to receive a handmade treasure. I know love is wrapped in the package.

When I reciprocate with a bought gift and add some love to the box, it never seems like an even exchange; inevitably, my conscience trips in. Then I think, "It's all right, maybe next year I can be creative."

Bride's Dress

A wedding that includes invitations, food, music, flowers, and the bride's dress is expensive. It makes many families ponder the extreme cost for the afternoon or evening event. One bride fell in love with a dress that was so expensive that the mother gasped. Then she and her daughter began to think. They bought the dress, but added a charitable twist. They decided to donate money equal to the cost of the wedding gown to favorite causes.

As the engagement year progressed, the mother and daughter found several special charities and sent away the checks. A wedding dress had triggered expressions of generosity.

Everyone's Invited

*I*f possible, in nursery and elementary school years, make generous moments by inviting the whole class to a child's birthday party. Many parents are overcome at the thought of twenty or thirty small people, each with two hands, two feet and busy minds romping around their homes. Perhaps, invite other moms to help you and keep it simple and short. Some children grow up never invited to another child's house for a party.

Even when it is necessary to shorten the class list, some invitations are a must. Remember to include any children who have already entertained your child at their parties. That's returning an invitation. A parent's generosity toward other children sets an example for the future behavior of a child.

"Everyone's invited" sounds good and feels good when you're a little child.

The Cousin Connection

Sometimes the relationships within one older generation fall apart and bridges within a family are broken, but their children still shake hands and hug. That's the Cousin Connection. Many cousin generations want to acknowledge kinship, savor friendship and ignore their parents' problems about what folks did and didn't do in the past. They don't want disappointment or anger to cloud their relationships.

In one family the cousins congregate yearly in the same place for dinner. They live fairly close to one another, but set aside one special night to nourish the Cousin Connection.

In another family, all the cousins gather yearly at different places. The cousins take turns making the unique arrangements. They have enjoyed family ski weekends, shared rented cottages, ventured together on a cruise, spread picnics by a favorite lake, and once it was a black tie dinner for a big cousin event. Their Cousin Connection thrives on friendship and good communication.

Keep the Cousin Connection. It's generous in spirit.

Birthdays

Remembering a person's special day is ever-appreciated, ordinary kindness.

It's wonderful to know friends', relatives', and neighbors' birthdays. Keeping track of everyone's particular day is one more list in a desk drawer or on the computer, but it's an important one. Make phone calls or send cards, e-mails or gifts. People like to be remembered on their birthday. It's their day!

One aunt couldn't remember individual birthdays, but once a year she would send a surprise. A package would suddenly arrive with everyone's presents and special cards attached. Great serendipity!

Another aunt decided to honor her husband on his birthday with a party each year, even after he had passed away. The invited guests knew it was Howard's birthday party. She placed extra pictures of him around the living room and when asked why she started this unusual tradition, she simply explained, "I celebrate George Washington's birthday and I knew Howard better."

Occasion for a Toast

Warmth radiates and bonds grow stronger when young and old participate at a gathering and express their sentiments in toasts. It is a chance to convey feelings of congratulations, appreciation, and admiration.

My aunt felt that no occasion would be appropriate without toasts from family and friends. In fact, she thought that as long as she rose in her elegant silk chiffon gown and spoke forth with enthusiasm, the ordinary party rose to a celebration. The simple gesture left a strong impression of a lady who loved family and loved life.

Add the cheer of thoughtful toasts. Think beforehand so your chosen words will bring joy and make the honored one feel good. Remember, kind words and not-so-kind words continue to be tucked away in memories long after they are spoken. Hosts, hostesses, brides and grooms, and folks with big birthdays will all appreciate a raised glass and wise, wonderful words.

Valentine's Day

*E*very day for a week before February 14, an office worker encouraged her boss to create a Valentine dessert for his wife. When the day came, he bought the few necessary ingredients: double chocolate, fresh plump strawberries, and powered sugar, and then he cooked the surprise. That night he heated the meal, opened the wine, signed his card and invited his wife to dine.

Overcome by the display, she quickly took a snapshot for the family album of the delicious strawberries dipped in chocolate arranged in the shape of a heart. What a special expression of devotion! It was their thirty-eighth Valentine's celebration together.

Halloween Photos

A road of fifteen houses changed quietly over a five-year period from a road of *old* to a road of *young* and energetic families. For years, very few Halloween ghosts and goblins knocked on the door for candy.

Then change burst forth. To interact and get to know the smallest neighbors, a longtime resident began to photograph the characters in their costumes, individually and with their parents. It's become a tradition and families look forward to the pictures documenting the year's unique outfits. Within days the photographic results are delivered to mailboxes for sliding into albums or desk frames.

As the *young* grow *older,* perhaps the photos will flash back memories of a friendly road on Halloween nights.

Sweet Surprise

"The market may rise, stocks may fall, but you will always have this present from me. Enjoy your Christmas."

This was the card on a lovely present wrapped in a little blue box in a little blue bag that arrived by mail from a nephew to his very surprised aunt. The silver bracelet was a magnanimous gesture of affection. She wouldn't be home with her extended family for the holidays and he wanted her to feel remembered.

Engraving Traditions

"Rachel came for Christmas 1992" was engraved on a small, silver bowl. The host family wanted to commemorate the beginning of a tradition because they intended to invite her for many Christmases to come. The tenth year, Rachel filled the bowl with dried cranberries and brought it on the train. She wanted everyone to see the engraving that verified a decade of Christmases had been celebrated together.

Rachel's presence was the best present of all. Including an extra friend every year in a family holiday magnifies the occasion and personifies kindness.

Generous Offers

Free Today
Promise for Next Year
Noticing the Less Noticed
Just a Quarter
Take Your Things
Make a List
Stay Long
Library Flowers
Volunteering
For a Daughter-in-Law
Connect People
To Please Another
The Long Shelf
The Ticket

Free Today

Generosity is when you ask how much you owe a storekeeper, friend, or stranger who stepped forward to help, and he or she replies, "Nothing. You don't owe me anything."

"Free today" happens every day. You do it for others; they do it for you: a gift of time, a quick repair, a generous moment. That's the Golden Rule in action, "Do unto others as you would like others to do unto you."

"Free today" is the spirit of goodness on an ordinary day.

Promise for Next Year

---

*E*ven when children grow into adults, the surprises keep coming.

"Attention, Dad, you are off the hook from now on. You've done it for your lifetime! No more climbing ladders, no more cleaning gutters, no more pulling the snow off the roof, no more shoveling, no more trimming the top of the tree. Call me or talk to Mother. And next December, I promise five hours or whatever it takes to get the house decorated."

That's a spontaneous gesture of generosity from a busy young man who does not want his dad to overdo.

Noticing the Less Noticed

On turnpikes and in airports, travelers see people cleaning the ladies' and gents' rooms. As travelers travel on to interesting places, the workers stay. Stopping there is only a moment, but it may be their whole day. It may also be the second, third, or fourth job they tend to weekly in order to house, feed, and educate their children.

When a friend sees the attendant on a weekend or holiday, she often hands her a little money and thanks her for being there. She has always seen surprise and heard appreciation, but she has also seen tears. Perhaps the one with tears was overwhelmed that of the hundreds who passed through her restroom, someone had noticed her and said, "Thank you."

Just a Quarter

"Do you need a quarter?" floated a voice across a parking lot as my husband and I tried to decide if we could chance leaving the meter empty for a quick trip into a store. Two cars away stood a woman with a roll of quarters *volunteering* to make a money exchange.

Having the right number of quarters in our pocket for parking meters, phones, laundermats, subways, buses, and vending machines is always a hope and a challenge. "Hope" because we hope we have brought the right coins and "challenge" because if we haven't, can we find money on the spot? At times "Do you need a quarter?" is music to our ears. The answer comes with a quick sigh of relief, "Yes, thank you very much."

Take Your Things

———

all home and tell your folks that you are ready to come pick up your old pictures, trophies, tee shirts, toys, schoolbooks, and all your memorabilia. Such an offer will rank high on the generosity list. Parents will be ecstatic. My children think that their things are more "at home" at our house, so why disturb them? I explain that cleaning out is inevitable and sooner is better than later. I'm still waiting for the phone calls.

Make a List

A thoughtful son called his mother, "If there is anything you want me to do when I come home, just make a list." What a wonderful offer!

Some children are born with the ability to repair things. When they marry and move away, their talent is sorely missed. After the son made his offer, the mother began thinking of ideas. A list of quick jobs grew: replace light bulbs in high ceiling, check squeaking doors, saw a limb, and connect a video player. She could picture instantly that she would talk and he would fix.

Projects done in the spirit of togetherness are always more fun.

Stay Long

An invitation to visit a friend arrived in the mail. It included a map and all the details. I knew immediately that I couldn't go, but what lingered longest were the final words, "Come early and stay long." What a sense of welcome! As the day approached, I thought of the gathering group and imagined what fun it would be to "Come early and stay long."

Library Flowers

A gift was recorded in garden club archives in the 1960s: "We should thank Marjorie Macrae for putting flowers on the reference desk at the library for two years." What devotion! Flower arrangements provided by one individual every week for two years.

The flowers had to be grown in her garden or bought and arranged and then required water and attention as they progressed from fresh to wilted. The containers needed be cleaned and changed for variety. And imagine the number of car trips she must have taken to the library to complete her obligation!

Only one sentence in the annual report doesn't seem an adequate tribute considering the extent of dear Mrs. Macrae's gift. At least now she is remembered in a book on generosity.

Volunteering

---

*V*olunteer. Rock newborns at a hospital, drive senior citizens, answer phones, play instruments at a retirement home, make food for a homeless shelter, mentor a child, or read to those who can't.

A friend reads inspirational stories every Monday at a given hour in a convalescent home. It is a peaceful time for the residents who attend the reading. Some are alert and enjoy the words while others find it a nice time to sleep.

Another friend likes to do her volunteer job at home. She collects fabric remnants that have been donated to a thrift shop and stores them in her garage. In her free time, she measures each piece, prices it, and then returns the remnants to the store ready to sell.

The list of ways a volunteer can serve others is endless and every age is needed. Volunteering is an outward expression of a generous heart.

For a Daughter-in-Law

*H*ow do you get to know the wonderful woman your son has just married? Invite her on a mini vacation and leave your husbands at home with the dogs!

A mother-in-law offered her new daughter-in-law a weekend trip and asked her to choose the place and the time convenient for her. When they discussed possible destinations and realized they shared a favorite singer, Memphis became the vacation site.

A few months later, off they went for three busy days. With so much to see and do and discuss, to their surprise, they seldom mentioned the special person they had in common, the son/the husband. There would be years to do that. On the trip they built a new relationship and returned home with happy memories.

Connect People

When a friend moves to a new area, contact old friends there and take steps to connect the new with the old. Share good things and important details. They already have knowing you in common and they can learn more when they meet.

It's very helpful for newcomers to have contacts in new places. Your generosity in locating the addresses and phone numbers and your making the connection can result in good friendships.

Recently an away-friend introduced me to a new acquaintance in town. When the woman and I had lunch together, we had our photo taken and put on a coffee mug as a gift for our mutual friend to show that we had finally met. Now she has coffee with the two of us smiling on the cup—a creative three-way connection.

To Please Another

*T*here were extra flowers after doing arrangements one Saturday morning. While chatting with a volunteer, I handed her a bunch of yellow tulips. "Please, take these. They're extra. Now they are yours." I really wanted her to have them. But she surprised me. Her face lit up as she said, "Oh, I'm going to visit my daughter when I leave and she loves flowers. Now I have a gift for her. You know, this makes my whole week above average. Things have been flowing in my direction!"

Imagine all this enthusiasm for handing a friend a bunch of tulips! They weren't even going to bring her pleasure; the flowers were going immediately to bring pleasure elsewhere. Our generosity depends on the size of territory devoted to love in our hearts. Hers is big.

The Long Shelf

*A*lways a question: What to do with children's and now grandchildren's hand-made creations? The answer: offer a special place for permanent display. Clay animals, sculptured bowls, hand-painted tiles, and small models are precious gifts. To a child, a present appreciated is a present seen every time he or she visits.

One family's solution was to build a long, narrow shelf almost the length of the family room for the artwork. The shelf has distinction, because it holds one-of-a-kinds. It has also been successful for budding artists who like to admire their progress from simple to more complex.

As yearly more gifts go on the shelf, discussions about the objects become lively conversations with guests and family members. The creations are always enthusiastically given, and they are generously admired.

The Ticket

A father drove his daughter to the airport for a business trip to New Orleans one late January. On impulse, the dad, an avid football fan offered, "If you can get a ticket to the Super Bowl, your brother and I will pay for it." She knew next to nothing about football, and her father was only half serious.

Imagine his surprise when the family was gathered around the television set and the phone rang as the Super Bowl Game was about to start. "I'm on the fifty yard line! Can you believe it?" They were stunned and began to imagine the experience vicariously; one of their own was in the stadium. Then she called at half-time in the middle of more excitement and the extravagant musical entertainment, "Oh, is this what football is all about? I love it!"

She, the only non-football enthusiast in the family, was at the game of games. Her father and brother had introduced her to the sport at the Super Bowl. It was her first football game. What a ticket!

Big Gestures
of Generosity

Fill the Wish List
Tons of Generosity
Banner of Love
Events for Others
A Generous Home
The Monthly Dinner
Birdhouses Make Music
The Best Break
Warm Visits
Flowers for Everyone
Goodness for a Dog
Syrup for Kindness
Gift to a Town
Gift of a Garden
The Photographer
Thanks and More Thanks

Fill the Wish List

Some people don't have as much good fortune as others. As much as they try to save, some expenses are beyond their budget. They never complain about their lives, but they may need help with buying a major purchase. If it is possible, give the gift. Write a check or provide the goods. Think of the anxiety lifted from heavy shoulders. To them, the gift means they can go on.

Or, to lift spirits, give a surprise that is something friends or relatives would love to have but would never treat themselves to: acting lessons, piano lessons, tickets to a play or a special sporting event, a short trip to somewhere or a day at a spa. Everyone has a different wish list.

If someone is having a difficult time, it may be within your power to give something that would brighten another's life.

Tons of Generosity

"Towels for Tanzania," a sixteen year old's Eagle Scout Project, was the result of a dinner conversation with a doctor-missionary priest on home leave.

The question: "What could one person do to help your hospital?"

The answer: "If you open your mother's linen closet, please give us any extra sheets and towels."

The simple exchange inspired a huge, year-long international relief effort that culminated in sending 15,000 pounds of towels and bedding from Connecticut to a 800 bed hospital in Tanzania serving 3,000,000 people.

Many were skeptical. But the young man raised $19,000 to pay for metal freight containers. He recruited family, friends, and volunteers to collect, weigh, and box the supplies on four Saturdays. The philanthropic organization, AmeriCares, agreed to ship the cargo to the front door of the hospital in Africa. So many hands helped.

When the boxes of towels, sheets, pillowcases, and blankets arrived, the patients and refugees were astonished. Their reaction was: Who are these people who care for us? They don't even know us!

Bravo to Bradford who linked people with extras to people with needs.

Banner of Love

As she awakened from surgery, words of encouragement were posted on the walls and ceiling of her hospital room. Friends from Bible study took turns sitting outside her door. They began a prayer chain and shared news of her progress. These acts of love went on for weeks and weeks as she slowly made gains on her challenge.

The doctors were overcome by the faithful vigil. One morning a doctor greeted one of the sitters, "How is our patient doing today? May I go in?" Friends simply wouldn't let her slip away. Today she is thriving and she remembers the amazing acts of goodness by her friends.

Events for Others

The training isn't easy, the routines are boring, it costs personal money, but many people arrange their daily lives to run, walk, bike, swim, climb, golf, or play basketball for good causes. They proudly wear the name of a stranger or carry the name of a loved one in their heart. Their efforts, sponsored by others, are an outpouring of generosity.

A father-son team has run marathons for over ten years. Together they have raised over $200,000 for medical research. That is quite a number! They can't stop, because they know by running for one day, they may make a big difference for others in their struggle to live every day.

Another young man swims rivers, crosses channels, strokes around islands and under famous bridges to bring the prospect of better health to those who suffer illnesses.

The spirit to help others is contagious. Friends enlist friends and whole families enter challenges together for important causes. Not everyone can make big gestures, but if you can, join the race!

A Generous Home

A supreme example of generosity is raising children. Perhaps twenty years of devotion and hard work are required according to the usual job description of Parenting. Children need a nurturing home, but the task often seems endlessly daunting when 365/24/7 is multiplied by so many years. The generous spirit of being a parent also means giving up much of our own self-orientation. While everyone continues to multi-task, busy homes with loving support offer children the best ticket for life's express ride.

After years of devoting time and energy and money, like birds, the kids will fly away, but the nest will draw them back if love has been the fire in the hearth. The supreme generosity of years spent raising children reaps the reward of having FAMILY forever.

The Monthly Dinner

What a lark! The third Thursday every month is Women's Night Out. What's unusual is that it's a mother-in-law's gift to her three daughters-in-law. She makes the arrangements at a different restaurant each time and pays for the evening and the necessary sitters. The four have a grand time catching up, and without the men-folk, the topics for conversations are all theirs.

You have probably guessed what happened. After a few months of the women having fun with their mother-in-law, the father decided to invite his sons to a Men's Night Out at the same time. The men have a few different rules. They sometimes include other men to fill in the gaps between conversations, and they always return to the same restaurant.

It has become a Not-to-Miss Night each month, for a mother-in-law, a father, three sons and their spouses. For one evening their lives slow down in the city and family ties grow stronger.

Birdhouses Make Music

A church needed a piano. A master craftsman stepped forward with a novel plan. He offered to buy the church the piano by selling birdhouses that he would build in his woodshop. The birdhouse design would be the exact to-scale replica of the church from steeple to front steps.

It was an exceptional project for an individual to undertake. Using marine plywood, stainless steel nails, glue and yachting enamel paint on every small piece, he constructed over 130 perfect birdhouses, guaranteed to be weatherproof for their inhabitants. After months of effort and a big sale, the craftsman's generosity made music for his church.

The Best Break

A doctor enjoyed helping young people and his gifts often impacted their lives.

When a sophomore in high school broke his leg at the beginning of the football season, he was devastated. Then, at the beginning of his junior year season, he broke the other leg.

The team doctor knew how much the young man loved sports and he gave him another option. "It doesn't look like you're supposed to be a football player. If you're interested, next summer I'll send you to camp to learn to be a sports trainer. Then you can help me with the teams next year."

This gift started the teenager on his future career path. He is now a physical trainer for a professional basketball team. It was the best break he could have had in his football career.

Warm Visits

When a mother was no longer able to live alone in her house, her three daughters decided on a plan of rotating four-month stays. Their mother's life was divided into seasonal visits in different locations where the weather was warmest, giving the mother variety and special time with each of her daughters. With planning and cooperation, the arrangement worked out nicely for everyone. The daughters' families opened their hearts and their homes, and the mother felt very lucky.

Flowers for Everyone

W hen the last member of a bridge group passed away at age ninety-three, relatives and longtime friends were invited to gather for a graveside service. The bridge ladies had bought their plots next to one another in a small cemetery decades earlier.

It was autumn in New England and someone had an inspiration. Place flower arrangements on the graves of all five bridge friends (there had always been a substitute), and on other friends' graves nearby as a way to remember them all.

Each elegant spray was created with an abundance of colorful roses in the center to offer a sense of formality. Then variegated greens and ivy extended outward as a natural transition between rose and earth.

The morning of the service, a gracious welcome of respect surrounded the granite monuments on the hillside. The minister and those assembled were overwhelmed with the sense of special families and the love that united them. The cemetery radiated friendship past and present. It was beautiful.

Goodness for a Dog

*H*ere, I must extend special thanks again to our own neighbor who carried our eighty-five pound, elderly golden retriever up the basement steps when we were away. Our family dog, Tag-along, went to the basement to find a cool spot and then decided not to attempt the return trip upstairs.

The young dog-sitter called us in panic and our hearts skipped a beat. Who could we call to lift Tagalong? A wonderful, strong, good neighbor! We will be ever indebted for his kindness to our dog on that day.

Syrup for Kindness

*T*he Sticky Syrup Company was started as a family project to encourage generosity when one family's children were very young. A couple in Vermont offered to sell small jugs of maple syrup to them at a low cost. The children in turn sold them to neighbors, family, and friends, making a small profit in the process. The arrival and distribution of the syrup caused great excitement. The children carefully delivered the jugs in their wagons and carefully collected the money.

As a company, the family agreed that the profits would be divided between three charities, and the children could keep ten percent. Meetings were called to discuss needy causes involving children. Then each child voted. From the beginning, The Sticky Syrup Company offered them a little entrepreneurship, a bit of responsibility, and a taste of generosity.

After a few years the maple syrup sale ended. The children grew up, but year after year, they have suggested and voted on favorite charities for the group to support. The Sticky Syrup Company continues to foster a special family experience.

Gift to a Town

*H*ow amazing that a small town post office could become a must-see attraction, in addition to the local historical churches and impressive parks!

A new postmaster transformed his workplace into a homeplace for his customers. Postal memorabilia, pictures handsomely framed, healthy green plants, organized display shelves, tables for writing, tidy counters, holiday decorations, and comfortable chairs all await the townspeople coming to buy and send.

The change in the building is astonishing. His generosity created a congenial atmosphere for everyone, and waiting in line is a treat because of the heart and efforts of one man, the new postmaster.

Gift of a Garden

*U*pon settling into her Japanese teacher's house, a young woman embarked upon a huge undertaking: building and planting an English garden for the people of a small rice-paddied village. Every day she worked hard on the tough dirt surrounding her house and the yard was slowly transformed. In three years she had created a blooming gift with roses climbing over a bamboo arbor, a tiny pond with a fountain, an herb garden, flower border, and brick terrace with a bench. Everyone was welcome in her quiet garden.

Curiosity about the American teacher who was building a "different" garden grew and while she was at school, people visited and always left a token: a tomato, an apple, bread, flowers, or seeds. Exchanging a gift for a gift. She was thrilled they had come to sit in her garden.

Although the woman has left the house in Japan, she hopes her small place of beauty, built with a generous heart, continues to attract visitors today.

The Photographer

A woman's gift has extended over twenty years and continues. She has been photographing every major event in the life of a church to build a picture history. Her beautiful albums sit in the front parlor for visitors and members to enjoy.

She has also photographed almost every flower arrangement created weekly by the flower guild for the altar. These albums have become reference books for arrangers to offer inspiration for weddings, religious days, and so on.

Each step in the process has been a valuable and generous gift: the cameras, film and developing, the leather albums, and the exceptional giving of her time, rain or shine, winter, spring, summer, and fall. Whenever she is asked, "How could you do all this?" she always smiles and quietly replies, "I just do it. I have loved doing it."

Thanks and More Thanks

Asked frequently if he would record his piano playing, an older relative continually resisted. Then grandchildren added their requests for a recording. The man eventually created a CD of twenty-five songs and dedicated it to his parents, his sisters, and his wife. It was no simple task. Although he played by ear, the project took months of planning. He had to select the best tunes from his repertoire of five hundred songs, locate the right sound studio, and then perform each song perfectly. Once accomplished, he had his own personal CDs for family and friends. Giant effort! Great gifts!

Recently, I called him across the miles to say that he was "at the piano in my home" and that I loved his music. He quickly replied, "You don't know how much this call has touched me."

The uncle really deserved to hear "Thank you" again. His present was so exceptional. Unless we speak up, others don't know our good thoughts and our gratitude for their gifts of generosity that continue to bring us joy.

Alison Buchanan
2000

Conclusion

W hile writing *Generous Moments* I became more aware of the special things people graciously do for one another. Each time I thought my writing was finished, I experienced another gesture that needed a page in the book. Being on the lookout, I found there is a never-ending supply of wonderful stories.

When friends hear of problems, what moves them to say, "Don't worry. I'll fix my schedule. What can I do to help you?" In spite of lives filled to overflowing with jobs and family obligations, kitchen duty and housework, exercise regimens and social engagements, people reach out to help one another in amazing ways. They all but move mountains for friends, family, and strangers. It's remarkable!

There are so many opportunities each day to affect the lives of others with kindness. Offering moments of generosity is as simple as sharing an umbrella with a friend or a stranger. Reach out and help create a generous world. When your heart sings, the echo will be goodness.

Alison Buchanan
May 2007

Snapshots of Generosity Around You

_T_he spirit of goodness is very much alive. Watch for it along the path; it happens everywhere. Then write your own special stories.

_____

_____

_____

_____

_____

_____

_____

_____

_____

_____

_____

_____

_____

_____

_____

_____

_____

_____

Generosity Exclaimed

Write it, say it, support it, express it, give it, encourage it, observe it, enjoy it! Generosity flows in many ways and takes many forms. Being generous is being kind and thoughtful. It shows respect. It shows appreciation for your own good fortune. Children, teens, adults, seniors, the well and the sick all know the difference between generosity and its opposite. It's the difference between closed hearts and open arms. Possibilities abound with the spirit of generosity.

Index of Moments

Alison Buchanan
November 1999